HOMECOMING

(Prologue)

Milo came home to me on a windy early fall Saturday. The sun was bright, and the temperature was a mild seventy degrees. I left work armed with a dog bed, his very first kennel, a lime green collar meant for a cat, and a disturbing amount of toys.

The important part about Milo's homecoming is how much I really shouldn't have had him at that time. I wanted him, of course. I needed him, but I didn't know that just yet. What I did know was that four months before I met Milo, I lost a big part of myself to addiction.

Now, I know what you're thinking; how did this girl get caught up in drugs? Well, this girl didn't... but someone I loved very much did. Without going too much into detail about myself, I lost a big love to heroin at twenty-four years old, lost a lot of weight and my will to live, and eventually my home. So when I met Milo, I didn't have four walls to call my own; I was freeloading at my parents' house.

I had moved home to recover, and that recovery didn't include a five week old dog, thank you very much. But Milo found me, and he chose me that Saturday afternoon. It's almost surreal to type this. In my mind, I see the four pound dog so clearly: his big brown eyes, his twisty brindle coat, that one white foot. I quickly snap back to reality when that white foot, now attached to an eighty pound body, lands in between my hands and begins to type.

It's been a wild ride, a journey in and of itself. And in the next pages, I'll tell you all about Milo and his puppy antics. The funny shenanigans, the "make you laugh until your sides hurt," nonsense. You'll also learn about our heartbreak, the setbacks, the days where I was convinced anyone in this world could raise this dog better than I do.

I suppose I spoiled the story a little bit, huh? You already know I didn't give up; he is sitting on me, after all. While adoption is always the best option, let's face it: adopted dogs come with their own struggles, a life we did not live with them, pasts we cannot erase and habits we wish we could escape.

The hard is what makes it great. I can tell you at least thirty times Milo has made me doubt myself, and I will. What

I can't tell you is the feeling when you get something right. The overwhelming feeling of pride you feel for a dog who finally feels comfortable doing the things a dog should do.

To tell you what that feels like is why I'm here. I'm supposed to be showing you how worth it adopting a troublesome dog and sticking it out really can be. So, I will try; try to capture love in a paragraph, inspire you to stick it out just one more day, and help you to understand that you are not alone in this world. There are a bunch of us dog moms in this world who know we are messing it up every day, but what we lack in decision making, we make up for in love and blind hope. (This is where I would chant, "one of us! One of us!" if I were talking to you right now.)

This book was written in the same

form as the blog which inspired it. No timeline, no filter and no censoring; no method to the madness. In its rawest and most open sense, this is us; a tale of two tails and the human they saved.

MILO'S IGLOO

When Milo was about three months old, I couldn't go to a room without him. Now, this includes the following me to the bathroom of course, but it also includes him howling outside the bathroom door if I managed to slip inside without my shadow.

One day, I took a shower and when I finished and started to dry off, I remember finding it odd that there was not a puppy staring at me, licking the water drops off my legs. I didn't have time to enjoy ten minutes without asking, "what are you doing, you little weirdo?" before the oddity of him not being there really sank in.

After finishing getting dressed, I

peeked into my room. No Milo there. Under the bed, in the closet, in his kennel, even inside his bag of Puppy Chow; no Milo to be found. My search went to the usual places in my parents' room, my brother's room, and the living room. Still, I had no Milo.

I will admit I started to panic. A three-month-old dog was missing! I walked around outside, calling his name, wondering how on earth a dog who cannot leave my side had wandered into the wild all on his own. My bare feet on the half-frozen November ground were the least of my concerns; a half hour had passed with no Milo.

The next step was the basement. No Milo in the dryer, in the second bathroom, or in the woodshop. He wasn't in the kitchen, the closets, or in the garage. At about forty-five minutes in, I started to cry. My first dog, my very first adult responsibility and I lost him. Who does that?!

Sitting on the couch scared out of my mind, I notice a ball of fluff behind the recliner. I got up to retrieve it, thinking, "his trail of fluff is all that's left of him." I was mourning a dog because I hadn't seen him in nearly an hour. Convinced he had met an untimely demise in the hour that I hadn't supervised him, I picked his fluff up and sat on the hardwood, taking the place of the destuffed toys.

I heard a sniffing sound, and when I looked up, I saw the tiniest brown eyes staring back at me. Milo had found himself bored and decided to tunnel into the back of the recliner in the living room. All I saw was a tiny Milo inside a hole in the chair, brown eyes looking back at me from an igloo of polyester and stuffing.

I think that was the moment that I realized I didn't get a so-called "normal" dog. Because in that moment, he didn't look rambunctious, or even guilty to be caught in the act. Rather, he looked... scared. To this day, I believe he dug into the furniture because he was hiding, not because he was being destructive.

While I wouldn't get a complete diagnosis until he was six months old, that tunneling incident should have been my first clue to his struggle with anxiety. And it would have been, but in that moment, I was so relieved to find him alive and well, albeit a little fluffier than he was before.

This book should be dedicated to my parents, if only for the recliner alone. They lived through Milo's puppy days right alongside me. Long after I left home, before Otis came to be, they even babysat a great number of times, just so I could go and have a life.

THE FIRST BAD VET…

Or the First Time That Vet Was Bad

The first time we ever had a bad experience with Milo's vet, he was six months old. I had called and explained to them that when left alone, he nervously chewed on his own feet, ate half the house, and barked himself hoarse. He was terrified of being alone, and not in a cute, "aww my dog loves me" kind of way.

So I make this appointment, take him all the way down there and what do they do? They tell me he's just a baby and that's how they act at that age. They tell me I am not hard enough on him, discipline him more. They say he acts

11

this way because I allow it, because I encourage it; basically anything to make it my fault and not a medical problem.

I knew deep down that normal dogs didn't act that way. They don't harm themselves in a panic when they realize they've been alone for mere minutes. They don't bark all day until they can barely make a sound just because no one is there to give them attention.

When I took him in, I mentioned that he had torn up some carpet as well. The vet focused on that and made it seem like all I cared about was the material side. Like I was wanting to medicate my dog because I didn't want my house to be messy. I could not have cared any less about the carpet, the couch, or anything in these four walls. I only cared about his happiness and well-being.

We left that day with no answers and no diagnosis. He was no better off than before I took him in, and I felt more like a failure than ever. Looking back, he had a bad vet, not a bad mama. In that time, in that moment, I couldn't differentiate between bad care and a medical professional who just would not listen.

At the time, I didn't think it odd that his vet never touched him, that he wanted him muzzled just for his breed, or that he never seemed to relax around his doctor. I was young and naïve, a brand-new dog mama, and I didn't know enough to stand up and demand better care.

Fortunately for us, by time he had his second run in with that vet, I knew more and had the nerve to speak up and change vets. But that's another story for another time… or another chapter, I should say.

MILO'S POTATO

It's surreal to be sitting here writing this. I mean, three years ago, I wrote about Milo and his potato, and I spoke to eight people. There are more than eight people at Easter dinner in my family, so talking to only a little more than half a dozen people was the definition of starting small.

Today, I write to thousands of people from all over the world. We have friends in Switzerland, Canada, France, and Mexico. There are people from just about every one of the fifty states in the country, and even people from down the street.

So now I'm this girl in Michigan

whose graduating class had barely one hundred kids, and now there's thousands of people who care what I have to say?! It's humbling, it's shocking, and it's unbelievable for me.

The original eight were greeted with a photo of a potato. A baked one at that. And no, it wasn't the typical Instagram type food photo, and it wasn't decorated with sour cream and chives. It was a photo of a half chewed up baked potato, taken at eleven at night in the half-lit kitchen.

You see, Milo has always had a slight attachment to his things. He doesn't have toys, per se. He has "babies." He carries his toys around and takes them to bed with him. When he wakes up, he brings them to the living room with him, and if you move them from his carefully designated places, he will hunt them down and put them back- even if the place he chose was in the middle of the walkway.

One night in March, he was whining at the bedroom door at bedtime. He scratched and whimpered until I opened the door for him to go get his ball or rope or stuffy, whatever it was he desperately needed for bedtime.

I was half asleep, so when he came back in, I shut the door and climbed into bed. A four-month-old Milo was too small to get into my bed alone, so he whined to be picked up. I picked him up, rolled over and quickly began to drift off.

I became more alert when I noticed that Milo was chewing on whatever toy he had. Not wanting to listen to a squeak or chewing noises, I reached down to take it from him. I expected a tennis ball. Maybe even a rope.

Instead, I got a handful of baked potato. And we hadn't had baked potatoes that night, rather the night before. This puppy had hidden his baked potato in a house with two other dogs, for twenty-four hours until he decided it was time to get it back out.

I had never read about shenanigans quite like the ones Milo performed. I read a lot online about dogs who can sense seizures, dogs who save people from burning buildings, and dogs who know sign language.

But where were the dogs who brought baked potatoes to bed? The dogs who stole cupcakes from the table, who hated baths so much they suddenly had no bones in their bodies? Where were the dogs like Milo, and where were the mamas like me? Why was no one talking about how hard it really can be somedays?

So I wrote. With the belief that I needed someone like me, I started writing to eight people in the hope that someone else could use a me. And three years later, I'm writing a book.

Pretty cool where we came from after starting with just a potato, huh?

FAT AND DRAMATIC

Perhaps the story that's the best known is the story of Milo and his official diagnosis of "Fat and Dramatic."

I told you I had another story about his vet, one that made me switch to a new provider, and here it is. Be warned, this may aggravate you. As a dog lover, which I'm sure you are since you're reading this, you'll be just as upset as I was at the care he was given.

When Milo was nearing two years old, I noticed he was getting quite hefty. During a checkup, I mentioned that I believed he had a bad thyroid. The vet dismissed me and said to feed him less and walk him more, and he would drop the pounds easily.

Stupidly, I listened to his advice even though Milo was a grazer who rarely ate more than a mouthful or two of food at a time. Despite the fact that the boys and I walked a route that spanned nearly six miles daily, I pushed him and made him do seven.

He was a two-year-old dog who could barely walk. He was panting by the half mile mark and his legs were twitching by time we made it home. Something was clearly not right, and I could feel in my heart that he had some-thing wrong with him.

Back to the vet we went, where his doctor told me to cut him down to a quarter cup of food A DAY. I put my foot down and said I refused to starve my dog, said I wanted the thyroid test done that day, and that I knew something was wrong with him.

Besides doubling his weight in less than six months, he also had ears so dry and itchy that they would crack open and bleed. "Just allergies," I was told. When I brought up his sudden misbehavior and pointed out that my wonderfully behaved dog refused to listen to me seemingly overnight, "you're not training him right," was the response.

It came to a head when I came home one day, and Milo was gulping down water like he hadn't drank in days. He was panting and could not seem to catch his breath, and I nearly had to carry him out the door because his little legs had given up on him.

I rushed him into his vet and after explaining again that something isn't right, I was told that two-years-old is not old enough for a thyroid condition. That my bad parenting of him caused him to be "fat and dramatic."

I changed to a new vet and called the old one for them to transfer the records of both boys. They asked if I was moving away or relocating, and I told them simply, "Nope, you guys wouldn't do what I needed, so I found someone who would."

I made both boys an appointment and got a blood draw done on Milo that day. It was also discovered that what his old vet called "allergies," was a severe ear infection in both ears causing his skin to split open and bleed. He suffered for months with bleeding ears because his vet couldn't be bothered to listen.

Thankfully after four days of ear drops and heavy antibiotics, he was all healed up and acted like a brand-new dog. Even better, after six days, the doctor called and confirmed what

I'd always suspected: Milo had a thyroid that barely functioned at all. His blood panels showed no discernible signs of thyroid activity.

We medicated immediately, and after a week on the pills, he had his energy back, He was running and playing and eating like a normal dog should. He bounced around the house, played in the laundry baskets, chased his tennis balls around. And in one month's time, he had lost an astounding thirteen pounds. After two months, he had dropped nearly thirty.

It's amazing to me how much life he lost simply because his vet wouldn't listen. All he had to do was listen and understand that I know Milo better than anyone in the world and take my concerns seriously.

Instead, he shrugged off my

thoughts and replaced empathy and common sense with indignation and condescension. From that day forward, I've not stopped asking questions. If I don't understand, I ask. If it doesn't seem right to me, I refuse treatment. And if I know he won't be comfortable and happy, I'll speak up on his behalf.

While it's a terrible thing that happened, and I wish it hadn't happened at all, I am thankful it helped me find my voice. The boys will always have exceptional care because I simply refuse to accept less for them anymore.

ADOPTING A DOG WHO DIDN'T WANT TO BE RESCUED...

When I realized Milo's separation anxiety wasn't getting better on its own, and his vet sure wouldn't help me, I decided he may benefit from having a brother or sister around to help ease the discomfort of me leaving the house each day.

I had put off getting him a buddy because I didn't want a puppy to train. I had just gotten through the puppy stage with Milo, and really didn't want to start over fresh with another dog.

It occurred to me after awhile that I

could adopt an older dog, because older dogs are always trained already, right? Wrong. I searched shelters with the vision in my head of a dog who would be eternally grateful to me for being his savior. A dog who would love me and snuggle close on the couch, loving his new life, playing with his new brother, all the things you imagine when you think of springing a dog from their prison of a concrete floor and a wire kennel.

Through the shelter visits, I met rambunctious dogs, quiet dogs, and everywhere in between. None quite seemed right to me, so I never took the next steps on those dogs. For months I searched; every online posting, every shelter I could visit, every ad on Facebook. Not a single dog seemed to be right for me, or more importantly, right for Milo.

One day in July of 2016, my mom and I visited a Humane Society. We flipped through photos of dogs, looked at their stats, their faces, their temperaments. Again, nothing seemed right. Then I saw a name written on the dry erase board behind the reception desk, a name I hadn't seen come across the computer-based file book of available dogs: "Kipper."

I asked the receptionist about Kipper, and she said, "oh, you don't want that dog." The thing about me, if you tell me I don't want something, it makes me want it more. Now I needed to know who this dog was, because something about him had me very curious.

They brought him out and he was the sweetest thing, but something still did not quite click. We left the shelter empty-handed, but on the way home,

I said out loud, "I just keep thinking about that little Beagle." It surprised even me; I hadn't realized I'd been thinking of him.

This part is going to sound ridiculous and I know that. You're going to think I'm full of shit and I don't blame you for that. But no lie, on the way home, a cloud was floating above the freeway and it was shaped like a dog with his tongue hanging out. And I knew that dog was meant to be mine.

When I took Milo to meet him, a young kid performing community service was walking Kipper. He allowed them to sniff each other once and then took him inside saying they didn't get along.

I spoke to the shelter director and told her I didn't believe it was a problem and asked for another meeting. She agreed and walked Kipper herself, and surprising to no one, they got along swimmingly. They ran and played and shared toys in the outdoor area. I knew this dog was coming home with me, and apparently, he knew, too; he jumped in the car and refused to get out.

As I signed the adoption papers and waived off the warnings of, "he's been adopted and returned twice," and "he's a bit difficult," Kipper sat in the car with my mom, a big grin on his face, enjoying his first taste of freedom.

First on the list was to change that name. Kipper wasn't a name I was fond of, and I already had a Milo, so logically, I changed his name to Otis. Secondly, we needed to get him to his new home. Unfortunately, my dreams of a well-adjusted dog who loved me instantly were dashed immediately.

A NOT SO HAPPY HOME

The first day Otis was home, he played with Milo constantly. They wrestled and tumbled and ran themselves ragged, stopping only for water and the occasional breather. Otis never came close to me, but it was easy to shrug off as being too excited to play with Milo. Afterall, I could see he was having tons of fun with his new brother, it made sense to ignore me.

At the end of the day, he was done playing, but he didn't come around. He sat on the floor while Milo lounged on the couch next to me. He would alternate between taking a small bite of food and running away to hide in a corner to eat it, and what is known as "survival feeding," where he would eat so quickly in fear of not having a second chance, that he would throw all his food up, most of it still whole.

The first week was very touch and go with Otis. If I raised my voice for any reason, he would hide. If I sang a song, he was hiding behind the toilet, if I dropped a pan, he was diving under the couch. He was a mess and a half, and everything terrified him.

Otis feared me more than anything. He would take food I offered, but only by quickly snatching it from my finger-tips and then eating it while hunched over, protecting it. Everything he did, he did out of fear. He ate in fear, he slept without resting, he stood on guard con-stantly.

Getting close to Otis was impossible. While I had raised Milo from five tiny weeks, Otis was raised on the streets for the first three years of his life. Remember when I said older dogs were always well trained and behaved? I learned to eat those words while Otis ate... well, everything.

In his fear and frustration, Otis turned destructive. Nothing was safe from his jaws; not the carpet, not the couch, the drywall, or electrical cords. He ate my clothing, my shoes, candles, chemicals, bars of soap. Basically, if he could get his mouth close to it, he chewed on it, I called Poison Control, rinse and repeat.

He chewed a hole in the carpet that was nearly five feet wide. He ate my beautiful sectional, and he peed on everything. Literally, there was not a thing he didn't feel the need to mark his territory on. He peed on the wall, on the furniture, on the counter, and on Milo on more than one occasion.

As Otis acted out, he pushed me further into a depression. My house was trashed, all my nice things were destroyed, I couldn't have any company in my house, and I couldn't afford to replace any of it. His first year was like this; I tried everything I could to train him, and he resisted all of it.

Otis didn't trust me, and I think that's where a lot of the disconnect came from. He didn't know any commands, didn't care to learn, and spent most of his time trying to run away from his new home.

I have always been honest about how hard Otis was on me. I contemplated day after day whether or not I should even keep him. The one time I came the closest to giving him away was Christmas Eve.

You see, I had worked about twelve hours, and it was, as always, the busiest day of the year for me. I came home to see that he had chewed a hole in the carpet I had recently laid to replace the carpet he destroyed.

I was livid to put it lightly. Here I was, staring at a hole in carpet I saved up four hundred dollars to have put down, and just days later, he ate it. I couldn't believe what I was looking at, honestly. A dream, I told myself. A nightmare that I'll wake up from soon.

That day, I cried. I sat on my TV stand and I sobbed. I swore and yelled and screamed until my voice was hoarse, and it didn't make me feel better. So, I called my mom and told her I was ready to take him back. Told her to just come get him and get it over with, tell the shelter I tried, and I failed him, just like so many others before.

Once she agreed, I backed down. I wouldn't know until years later that she planned to take him to her house and hold him for a few days, just long enough for me to regret giving up on him. She knew he was meant to be here and knew I would soon understand that.

We did get better, although it took a lot of time to learn to live with each other. He hated me, didn't trust humans in general, and I was not exactly fond of him either. He sensed I didn't like him, and I think that reflected in his behavior. The more I resisted him, the more he acted out.

Jeccika Shepherd

OTIS PICKS A FIGHT HE COULD NOT WIN…

On February 17th, 2017, Otis picked his first fight. I knew he had a long list of faults, but I didn't know dog aggression was one of them. He had been a little rough in the past, but never showed out-right aggression.

I remember that day so vividly, despite it being two years ago. My sister was getting married that fall and I needed to try on dresses. As I was in the bridal shop, I got notified that Aries and Otis had fought, and Otis had a scratch on his face. My dad had put him in the garage so he could rest and not be bothered by the other dogs.

When I got there to pick up Milo and Otis, I went straight for the garage where I yelled to my mom, "his face is hanging off!" The white shirt I had under my polo was covered in his blood, and I was sobbing already. This dog, a dog I didn't even like, was hurt and I was heartbroken.

We rushed him to the emergency vet and finally understood what was happening: his face was ripped so cleanly that it looked like a scratch to my dad, but as he moved and wiggled around, it opened up the rest of the way and the severity of his wounds was apparent.

When we got him to the vet, it was about nine at night, and I had been up since five that morning. I was exhausted, both physically and emotionally. While I sat on the floor of an exam room holding his face together with my hands, they were asking me for a debit card. Before administering any pain medication, before debriding the wound, they wanted the full amount of what they estimated an injury like his would cost.

I remember being so angry in that moment. How dare they let him sit there and bleed, sit there in pain, and care only about money? Thankfully my mom was there and took care of it. They estimated his surgery would be over a thousand dollars, and I had about two hundred in the bank. If she wasn't there, would they have denied him treatment? Let him sit there and bleed?

Another reason I was so angry with the vets, they subtly suggested euthanasia for Otis. I was told, "he may never look the same," and "he may be disfigured." They mentioned the cost and the fact that he may end up scarred and de-formed from the reconstruction.

I didn't care. There was never a second that I thought, "oh, if he's not perfect cosmetically, I'll just put him down." He meant more to me than being cute, more than a thousand dollars, and more than possible disfigurement. I signed the papers, got him examined, was told he would need ten to twelve stitches, and sent him in for surgery.

In that moment, I reached out the friends we had made by writing Michigan Juju. I was honest and told our friends what was going on, how much it would cost, and they took care of it. In a mere thirty minutes, our friends had raised almost $1,500 for a dog they did not know.

Six months after being adopted, this little Beagle had made such an impact on people's lives that they were willing to reach into their pockets and help pay for his medical care. People who did not know him and likely never would, reaching together to save him just because they believe in the good of people. To this day, I'm humbled and amazed at the generosity of strangers.

Half an hour later, the vet came out and told me he was fighting sedation. He was fighting the techs, the medication, and anything else they tried to do for him. She asked me to come back and talk to him, see if my voice would calm him down. I tried to explain that Otis didn't much care for me, that he had fought from day one just to get away from me.

I went anyway and spoke to him as they put him to sleep. He eventually let the sedation work, and he went to sleep as I went to wait for him. As they did the surgery, they found the damage to be much more severe than originally thought. While they estimated ten to twelve sutures, it ended up being around eighty. He had ripped his face open through four layers of skin and muscle.

The original puncture was centimeters from his right eye and his sinus cavity. He narrowly escaped permanent damage to his vision and breathing, somehow only suffering cosmetic damage.

When he came out, I didn't recognize him. He was bruised and swollen, missing hair on his face. He looked like Frankenstein with all the stitches sticking out of his face. The left side of his face was white and freckled, normal as could be. The right side, however, was dark purple, bloody and so swollen his eye wasn't opened all the way.

I shared photos of his injury and surgery site on Michigan Juju, but chose not to include the photos here. They're graphic and not the way I want you to know Otis. I want you to know his big brown eyes, his perpetual smile, and his freckled nose, not the graphic and heart-breaking stitched up face I knew for about two weeks.

When he came out of surgery, he couldn't walk straight from the seda-tion. He surprised me when he leaned his weight against my calves and used me to support him as he walked. For the first time, he was trusting me not to hurt him and not to let him down.

His injury helped us move past our issues with each other. Suddenly over-night, he was laying near me. Maybe not like Milo, but close to me, a single paw touching my shoulder to let me know that he was still there. He suddenly decided I was worthy of his trust, and while he opened up a lot, he still had a lot to learn about being in a family.

I have always believed he let me in that day because I didn't leave him there in that emergency vet's office. All his life, he had been given up on. People left, they walked away, and he spent his life bouncing between shelters and animal control, being adopted twice and returned as many times.

But in that moment, I didn't leave him. For the first time in his life, he was brought to a building with someone, and when he came out, they were still there waiting for him. For the first time, a human had come into his life and didn't hurt him, didn't let him down, and that showed him it was okay to love.

If you're wondering, he didn't end up disfigured by any means. He has a large scar where the hair doesn't grow, but the hair next to it grows and covers it nicely. If you know where to look, you can place your finger just below his eye and trace the rough scar tissue down to his chin.

He looks the same to me, and most people can't believe it when they see the photos of what he looked like that day. He is scarred, he is imperfect, but he is loved. And that day, he learned that he is capable of loving in return, and that's a miracle in itself.

MILO AND OTIS SAVE THEIR MAMA...

FROM... LOU BEGA?

In Michigan, it gets cold in the winter. Like, snot freezing to your face, hurt your skin when the wind blows, door handles frozen shut cold. To combat this cold, I would occasionally take a nice, hot bath.

This day was no different, and I loaded the tub up with bubbles and extra hot water. I soaked and relaxed as music played in the background. The boys were milling around, occasionally running by with a tennis ball or a squeaky toy.

As I got ready to get out, I decided to drain the tub as I sat in it, therefore saving the shock of cold air to warm skin.

The water drained and the dogs began to bark. They have multiple barks, and I can tell without looking whether they are playing or upset, whether they are hungry or needing to go outside.

This bark was upset and frantic, the kind that says, "mom, someone is in the house with us!" I sat naked in the bathtub, trying to hold the shower curtain to preserve what little dignity I had considering I was resembling a walrus in a rapidly draining bathtub.

I pictured my imminent death as the intruder (who was clearly in my house based on their barking) found their way to the bathroom. I pictured emergency personnel finding me curled like a baby rhinoceros in an empty bathtub, judging the amount of bath products I own.

In that moment, I suddenly realize I need to clean the toilet and I didn't

want the firemen and paramedics
to see my gross bathroom. There
couldn't be a murderer in my house;
I hadn't mopped the floor!

I noticed the boys were in the bathroom with me barking, not at either
door. Maybe they were scared, too? Or
maybe nothing was in the house, and
we faced no danger at all. So, what
exactly had them worked up and snarling?

They were barking at my speaker,
one that was playing a mix of 90's
music. The song? "Mambo No. 5" by
Lou Bega. The opening line his him
talking, saying, "ladies and gentlemen,
this is Mambo Number Five!"

To test my theory, I restarted the
song, and as they heard the man's voice,
they lost their shit. Barking and snarling
at the speaker, backing up to me to pro-

tect me from the obvious threat. They were convinced a strange male voice meant danger, and they were frantic with trying to find where it was coming from.

In the end, I was saved from a 90's crooner, the potential embarrassment of being found naked in my bathtub, and we switched the music to something they were more accustomed to.

It's been over two years, and we still have not played that song in my house. Experiences like that have a way of ruining a song for you.

GRAMMA HAS A MEAN NEIGHBOR

My mom has a mean neighbor. Not to people or kids, but to certain breeds of dogs that she deems "undesirable." And we all know which breeds those are.

So one day, Milo was maybe five months old, and across the street comes Carol. Fuckin Carol. "I just think you should know there's a Pitbull running around." I know Carol, he's mine.

"You never can be too careful with those dogs," she spat with spite. "You never know when they'll just attack," she whispered while side-eyeing my five-month-old dog.

Being that this woman was the one who came across the street to tell my parents when they moved in that she didn't like the color they were painting the living room, I already knew this woman would be trouble.

My mom is a nice lady, a classy lady, and does her best to keep the peace. Because of this, and only because of this, I have resisted the urge to tell Carol where she can stick it.

Resisted the urge to scream dramatically, "there's a vicious dog running loose, Carol, call the authorities."

Because I love my mom and don't want to complicate her life, I behave myself, even if biting my tongue is quite difficult. I keep the peace for her sake, but every time I see that woman, I want to be mean.

To this day, I see her pulling her curtains open to watch Milo when he's walking around in the yard. See those judging eyes glaring from the sheer curtains, wondering when my peaceful pup is going to maul her face.

WHO RESCUED WHO?

I spoke a little about how Milo was a risky bet; I adopted him at a time when I could barely take care of myself, let alone a tiny month-old puppy. But I adopted him, and it was the best choice I ever made for myself.

Milo gave me a reason to get out of bed every day. A reason to take care of myself, a reason to get out of the house and take walks. He, a five-pound puppy, held the weight of my sadness on his shoulders and helped me cope.

When I was crying and couldn't bring myself to get out of bed, he snuggled into my chin and stayed with me. Not playing, not doing much of anything. Simply existing, just being and relaxing and breathing. His little heartbeat would syncopate with mine, and I could feel myself calming down.

After a bad day, a day where my mind was attacking me, I would come home to a little dog with big brown eyes and crooked little teeth, and in his eyes, I felt at home. Sometimes we would play or go for walks. Sometimes, we would curl up in bed and sleep off the bad day. And sometimes, we would sit together on the couch, just breathing and being.

No matter what we decided to do, Milo was a saving grace for me. He really helped me learn how to love life again, and I laughed for the first time in ages while watching him bound around on his little puppy legs. I would throw the ball and laugh as he slid all over in his desperate scramble to catch it.

Unfortunately, as good as Milo was for me, it wasn't enough. I was still broken and sad, still hated life and myself, and I couldn't figure out why. While I struggled with my mental health, Milo struggled with his anxiety.

Milo had landed on a plateau and wasn't improving. He got better, then he stayed the same, stagnant and stuck in a rut. He wasn't getting better on his own, and I was at a loss for what to do to help him.

So, I did the thing I had vehemently denied any interest in doing; I adopted him a dog. And we all know how well that went.

I spoke earlier about Otis and how much trouble he was when he was adopted. Something I didn't touch on was how hard his behavior was on my mental health. My house was a destroyed and I hated coming home. I was miserable and lonely and didn't want to be around anymore. I was stuck in a life I didn't want, and there didn't seem to be a way out.

I spoke openly on Michigan Juju about my battles with mental illness, and I've never regretted that. When I opened my life and decided to be honest, I got message after message thanking me for helping people see in them what had been missed too long. The signs I mentioned were being overlooked and written off as a bad day, when, in reality, those people needed help, too.

There came a time where I was at my lowest and decided to stop existing. I decided the world would be better off without me, and me without it. I told my mom to take care of my dogs, and I swallowed a handful of pills with hope of escaping the pain I'd felt most of my life.

But as I sat on the floor of my living room, I looked at the worried faces staring back at me. Four big brown eyes looking at their mama as she cried on the floor, not understanding what was wrong. And I decided in that minute that I didn't want to leave them. I didn't know that I could rest knowing anyone else had them. What if no one else was patient and kind? What if they didn't know their favorite treats or how to clip their nails? What if they gave up on Otis and gave him away?

So I made myself throw up, and in that second, I believed that the four eyes staring back at me were the only ones who needed me. The only ones who gave a shit if I were alive or not. I was wrong, of course, but thankfully that was enough. Believing even two little creatures cared about me was enough to keep fighting.

Ultimately, I was diagnosed with major depression and a panic disorder. I got medicated and did so much better, but not without the help of the boys.

They got me out of the house to enjoy the sunshine. They would bring me their favorite stuffy toys and snuggle close at night. Their love is what helped me keep going long enough for the medication to start working.

Being medicated helped me be a better mama to the boys as well. They got more walks, more attention, and more patience from me. Their antics that once made me infuriated and had my flying off the handle now made me laugh. Their silly behavior that I never had time for was the highlight of my day. I made time to play and to wrestle, to keep their home clean and safe, and we went on at least two walks a day.

I spent a lot more time awake and a lot more time with them. They began to behave better because they were given more attention and love. They were happier because I was, and their actions reflected their new-found comfort.

It really makes me think about who rescued who. I mean, sure, I adopted them both and gave them a taste of the good life. But they saved me. From depression, from myself, and from a world that had long since forgotten me. I may have fed them and gave them comfort, but they showed me the good in the world that I had forgotten.

I never imagined that five-pound puppy growing into my confidant and caretaker, and I never foresaw that scrawny little Beagle becoming a primary reason for my continued fight for life.

I'm so glad I took a chance on them both; who knows what I'd be, or even if I'd be if I didn't have them.

Jeccika Shepherd

FINDING JOE

On Michigan Juju, I often chronicled the frustrating, hilarious, and defeating act of dating in your 20s. I had been on what felt like a million first dates and almost no seconds. And after about three years of being single, I had all but given up on dating.

Something I hadn't considered was that someone who was right in front of me may have been perfect for me. Someone I'd talked to a thousand times, spent breaks with, and became friends with over a period stretching almost two years.

There were so many times I would sit with Joe, the unassuming and kind

Jeccika Shepherd

man who worked with me. I would sit and complain about the day, about dating struggles, and about the boys and whatever shenanigans they were into that day.

One day, I started to look at him a little different. It was raining and I sat next to him on a picnic table outside. I slid over close and sat leg to leg to avoid being rained on, and I swear I think he stopped breathing for a minute. I had never looked at him for what he was; thoughtful, kind and smart. I had only seen the guy I worked with.

I decided I was going to get his attention, so logically, instead of asking him out like an adult, I decided to do it on the sly. First, I "accidentally" kept nudging his foot with mine under the table. This did not compute with him, so I had to bring out the big guns.

66

I spoke loudly in front of him about how the people texting me were never the people I wanted to be talking to me, and I got radio silence. Since I was going on vacation for nine days, I asked if he had a Facebook. He doesn't, and I coyly asked, "what if you miss me while I'm on vacation?" To which he replied, "I'll just have to wait until you get back, won't I?"

I could tell this was a lost cause, but I am stubborn. At one point, I was talking to him, took a pen from my pocket, and drew a little heart on his hand. That same day, I wrote my phone number on a piece of paper and handed it to him. I told him, "in case of emergencies," with a wink.

Two days later, I saw him, and he waved to me. I said, "nope," and went to walk away from him. He asked me what the matter was and if he'd done something to upset me, and I explained in very clear terms that I gave him my phone number and he didn't use it, and it hurt my feelings. He told me he didn't use it because he didn't have any emergencies. It was clear I was not dealing with any old guy here.

I stood in front of my friend and I said, "I like you, okay? I wanna go out with you, and I want you to like me, too." His face lit up, and we agreed to go bowling the day after next.

On our first date, he eased my mind a little. He told me he went home the day I drew on his hand and stared at that little purple heart for hours. He washed his hands carefully so as not to remove it and wondered repeatedly what it meant.

When we bowled, I kept catching

him staring at me, then shyly looking away. I gave him a big hug and he hand hovered me! I pushed his hands to my waist and told him it was okay to touch me. He seemed nervous, and after the bowling we went to get some dinner.

The world got dark around us, and suddenly we had been on a date for six hours. We went to a park and sat and talked for hours about anything and everything that came to mind. It was here that I learned he had almost as many siblings as me, that he had wonderful taste in music, knowing almost every song on my playlists. I learned that while he was nearly thirty, he had never had a serious relationship, and it occurred to me that he likely had never kissed anyone.

So, in that park, sitting on an old oak bench, I kissed him. In that moment, my whole world stood still. I knew, right then that I wanted him to be my last first kiss. I wanted this man to be my everything, and I wanted it now.

As we continued to talk, I learned he had liked me far longer than I had ever imagined. He told me about the day he started working for the same company, and he mentioned the orientation group he was in. They used to bring them around to talk to some of the managers and ask what we would recommend and advise to help them succeed. I remember telling them the same thing I told every group: buy good shoes, be on time, and never let me hear you say something isn't your job.

Little did I know, he remembered it, too. For over a year, he would take the long way around the store to pass by and see me. He would plan his break times to be outside with me so we could talk, and he watched me when I thought the world had forgotten me.

Of course, I asked him why it took me hitting him over the head with a sledgehammer called subtly to get him on that date with me, and what he told me broke my heart. This funny, smart, kind and thoughtful man had never asked me out because he thought he wasn't good enough for me.

He told me he stared at my phone number and racked his brain for hours to think of something about him that was good enough to get my attention and couldn't find anything, and that's why he didn't text or call me. He thought it was a joke, thought that he wasn't good enough for my attention or admiration.

We spent the next months trying to

get as much time together as possible. We would stay out most of the night, deprive ourselves of sleep, just to get a few more minutes with each other. It was the very definition of the honeymoon phase, and I loved every minute of it.

One of my favorite memories was in a different park, one that I drive by daily now. As I said, he was not exactly experienced with the opposite sex, and his hesitation showed. As we sat on a park bench, he kept looking down my shirt. Because of who I am as a person, I flashed him a peek of my bra.

He got a little more confident and asked if he could touch me. He ran his fingertips over my chest, and just as he went for the full groping, a kid walked around the corner with a flashlight.

I've never laughed so hard in my life, and the ride home was one of the best times we had together so far. In the best example of our personality differences, I was laughing so hard I was in tears, and he was mortified. He eventually laughed it off, but it took a good while for him to see the humor in it.

The biggest step for us was me allowing him to meet the dogs. He had picked me up from work on this thirtieth birthday, and we got a pizza to have a picnic at our park. The long talk park, not the exhibitionism park. Well, as his birthday is in July, it was blistering hot outside and our plan for a picnic was squashed quickly.

We sat in the car with the air conditioning on full blast and ate pizza. We watched the sun set over the river, and as the evening wore on, I told him I had to get home to the boys. He drove me home, and as I was getting out, he asked to meet them. I had put it off because I had such terrible luck with men that I didn't want to bring someone in their lives that wouldn't be around, and I told him that.

He brushed off my concerns and assured me he didn't plan on going any-where. So, I leashed up the dogs and warned him from fifty feet away that they bark, but they wouldn't hurt him. They're always leery of new people, al-ways having to put the protection mode on.

Imagine my absolute shock when they ran to him and began kissing his face, jumping on him, and loving him like they'd known him forever. They never acted like this, save for their fam-ily. Seeing them love him instantly so-lidified my feelings for Joe. Dogs are the best judge of character, and they approved, so he must be okay.

He had spent a few nights with me off and on, but the day they found pre-cancerous cells for the first time, I called him and asked him to come over. I told him I needed him, and he didn't ask any questions, just showed up. He came with a duffle bag of clothes because I told him he may want to spend the night, and he never spent a night without me again.

A lot of people side-eyed the situation. Some people thought we were moving too quickly, some laughed when we decided to move in together. But we knew, without the slightest hint of doubt, that this was right. I had never felt a love like this before, and it surprised me that my quiet, unassuming coworker was the one to give it to me.

In October, he gave me a beautiful

half-carat diamond ring and asked me to be his wife. In the little park where we would sit when we couldn't bear to see the night end, in our own little secluded spot, he got down on one knee and promised me the forever I never believed I'd ever find.

A few months from writing this, I'll take his last name, and we will begin to build a life and a marriage. Joe loves the boys as much as I do, and I couldn't imagine anyone better for me, or them, than him. We got lucky when he found us, and we plan to hold on to him as long as he wants.

OTIS AND MY SOCKS...

When I adopted Otis, I had no idea the bottomless pit I was bringing home. People always told me it's hard to raise a Pitbull, but those people clearly have never tried to raise a Beagle. Raising Beagles is not for the weak of mind, heart, or stomach, and I've learned the hard way how much of a challenge they can be.

It began when he ate the carpet and the couch. I wrote those off as bad manners since he had never had a home. Then he would chew on electrical cords, drywall, and doorknobs if he could reach them. He would steal the sticky fly ribbons that hung from the ceiling in the summer and eat everything but the thumbtack that held them. I still don't know how he got them down.

He ate dandruff shampoo, sucked on a bar of Irish Spring soap, drank Febreze. He ate a sponge, pooped confetti made of crayons, and snacked on deodorant. I had teeth marks in my toothpaste, picked up poop with shreds of tennis ball in it, and saw him cough up what I'm almost positive was rope.

The dog has eaten wood, cardboard, and paper. He eats poop, licks roadkill if he has a second, and has on more than one occasion licked the carpet until he coughed up hairballs. He's eaten a rotisserie chicken, including the bones, the label holding it closed, and half the plastic top.

I've given him the Heimlich Maneuver once. He swallowed a plastic squeaker whole and it lodged in his throat. While the Heimlich didn't work, I managed to dislodge the plastic by smacking him as hard as I could on the back, between the shoulders until it came flying from his mouth. And when it did, he tried to eat it again.

Poison Control knows me by name, their vet probably screens my calls by this point. I have begun so many conversations with, "hey there, me again," or, "hi, this is Milo and Otis' mom..."

The one thing in nearly three years I'd never seen this dog do is vomit. I think when he had his face ripped open and had all those stitches, he may have whimpered once or twice, but that was all. He doesn't show pain, doesn't show exhaustion, and he doesn't allow us to see when he's hurting and needing help.

A headstrong dog, he's used to being alone, and asking for help still comes a little slower than most dogs in his position.

So, when he climbed on my lap and snuggled, I knew something was wrong. He isn't a snuggler, not by any means. For all his wonderful traits, Otis is just not an affectionate dog, and after nearly three years, I have given up hope that he ever will be. When he climbed up and laid his head in my lap, I felt his ears were hot, a sign of a fever. In all this time, he's never been feverish. Milo is the sickly one, Otis is always a picture of health.

I told Joe how much this development worried me, and we kept an eye on him the rest of the evening. When we got up to do the last potty break of the night, Otis didn't want to go. The thing you should know about Otis, it doesn't matter if he's been outside ten minutes ago, he wants to go outside. He will pull and lunge and act like he's never seen grass in his life, so for Otis to refuse to go outside was concerning to say the least.

When we come inside, we always give the boys treats for going potty. Otis rarely lets us get inside the front door before plopping himself down in front of his treat cabinet in anticipation of goodies. We brought Milo inside and did his treat, and called for Otis to come and get some bites. He didn't want treats, either. Now this was panic-inducing. This dog always wants food, even if he's just eaten. *Especially* if he's just eaten. Refusing food of any kind was just not him.

As we went to bed that night, he curled up against my stomach. Sleeping with us is not his first choice as he gets overheated too quickly. We both acknowledged how weird it was that he was acting this way and discussed taking him to the vet. It's really hard to explain to the vet, "I need him to be seen because he's acting like a normal dog, and for him that's not normal."

We decided to keep an eye on him for the night and take him in first thing in the morning if he hadn't perked up. He laid down and snored, and I woke up every twenty minutes or so to check on him.

When I got up at five in the morning to go to a meeting at work, he wasn't himself. He was walking weird, and when he jumped on the couch with me, he whimpered. I petted him with one hand and started dialing the emergency vet with the other, and suddenly, he started gagging and wheezing.

In one smooth motion, he threw up on my legs, and what comes out but a whole no-show Hanes women's sock. A black one, if you were curious. He hadn't so much as chewed it, and I'm not entirely sure how he managed that one.

Once he got the sock up, he laid there panting and catching his breath for a few minutes. No more than five minutes later, he was eating and drinking like normal, and his behavior changed almost immediately.

I'm a worrier, so I watched him a while longer, and called the vet anyway. They told me how lucky he was to be able to remove the obstruction himself, as most dogs must have surgery to remove socks they eat. The vet told me if he hadn't gotten it up himself and it began moving down his intestines, we would have to have exploratory surgery done to find the sock and remove it to prevent blockage.

I'm thankful that he was able to vomit and remove the sock, and I'm thankful that he broke out of tough guy mode, even for just a minute to let us know he needed us. Maybe there's hope for him after all. Maybe he will become the affectionate and loving dog I always imagined him to be. For now, he's just fine the way he is. He's loving us the best way he knows how, and when push comes to shove, he knows when to ask for help when he needs us most.

Today's Kibble and Yesterday's Garbage:

OTIS GETS A TASTE OF HIS OWN MEDICINE...

We've already talked about how Otis is aggressive to other animals and how detrimental that has proven to be for him over the years. While he had gotten better about his aggression and had stopped attacking dogs, we still did everything we could to keep him away from any other animals.

When we went to the dog park and saw that the large dog area was occupied with two other dogs, we yelled that we would take the small dog area and proceeded to the gate. Thinking I had a perfect solution by going on the other side of the fence, we kept on our original plan to let the boys run in the small dog area until the other dogs vacated and allowed us to use the large dog space uninterrupted.

In the blink of an eye, the male dog broke through the gate and picked Otis up by his neck. He shook him and snarled as his owners tried fruitlessly to get him off Otis. He had Otis pinned to the ground and unable to fight back, and I held his leash helplessly watching as my baby got attacked.

In the span of seconds, I imagined what my life would be like if I didn't get the fight broken up in time. I pictured the little urn that would come home with me, and I pictured how lonely and quiet my house would become. I thought about how if I hadn't domesticated him and trained away his aggression, maybe he'd be fighting back right now. Maybe he would have stood a chance if I hadn't clipped his wings by making him a friendly dog.

Suddenly, the dog let go of Otis and turned his sights on the much bigger Milo. He bit Milo once in the head, saw he was dangerously outmatched, and returned to Otis, who he picked up by the face. I watched helplessly as my little buddy was swung through the air by his cute little face. His big brown eyes closed to prevent being bitten, his little body hanging limp as he went on a ride.

I did the only thing I could think to do, and it's something I'm still ashamed of today. I drew my foot back, and as hard as I could, right square in the ribs, I kicked that fucking dog. I felt my foot connect with his ribs and stomach, and I knew I got his attention.

He let go to turn his attention to me,

and I picked up Otis and ran. As Otis struggled to escape, his fight returning, I held as tight as I could. He wiggled and I grabbed a leg, telling myself I could cast his leg if he broke it, but I couldn't let go and let him get killed. I held on tight as he scratched and bit at me to be released, and soon enough, the other owner had her dog back under control.

As I caught my breath, the other people left with their dogs, and I never once thought to exchange information in case of injuries. Otis seemed fine, after all, so what was the point in getting names? The only thing that mattered was getting the dogs away from each other and safe from another fight happening again.

I later noticed that Otis had a deep puncture wound in his face. He had multiple teeth marks in his neck and

under the roll of fat Beagles have to protect them from coyotes and other animals who may harm them while out
hunting, something they were bred for.

Social media can be a wonderful
thing, and it proved to be an asset to us
that day. I posted looking for the owner
and made it clear I wasn't looking to de-
monize their dog, I didn't want to press
charges, and I didn't want to take their
dog away from them. I had one simple
question: was their dog vaccinated? Because if not, I would have to have Otis
boostered for Rabies and other diseases
that he may have been in contact with.

In just a few hours, I was contacted
by the woman who owned the dog,
and thankfully he was fully vetted. We
got lucky and weren't exposed to any
viruses or illnesses because they were
good dog parents and vaccinated their
dog, too.

Otis got a taste of his own medicine that day. He was suffering for a day or two with a bruised ego, and his face healed up just fine. I think between being attacked and losing, and the time he attacked Aries and lost, it may be safe to say that Otis is becoming much more docile. While I wouldn't ever trust him around other dogs he didn't know, I have hopes that maybe we will have an easier time one day.

Maybe you can take the fight out of the dog.

THE DOG WHO
WAS ALLERGIC TO
THE WORLD

Milo was raised from five weeks old, so logically he should be in perfect health, right? Wrong.

Milo is a sickly dog, and if he could catch it, he did. If there was something that he could be allergic to, he is, and if there was an issue he could have, boy did he have it.

We spoke about his issues with being alone, but that was just the start of his health problems. Besides his failing thyroid, he was also cursed with being allergic to the world and everything in it.

His biggest allergy is flea saliva. No, he has never had fleas, and no, my home has never had them, either. But in Michigan, we have sand fleas, rotten little parasites who live in the dirt and the grass, waiting to pounce on a dog and bite it.

What most people are not aware of is the fact that most flea and tick preventatives are only affective when the flea bites. While it kills the flea and prevents infestation, it does little for dogs like Milo who are allergic to the saliva and react to a single bite.

I took Milo to the vet to address some skin issues and found he was having problems with fleas again. He had itched his skin to the point of bleeding, and his lower back by his hips was hairless most of the summer. Nothing seemed to work to get him to leave it alone, and while he would whimper each time he scratched, he couldn't seem to stop itching the raw and bleeding area.

I chose to put him on steroids to try and help the itching, and he had an allergic reaction to the steroid shot, making his skin condition worse. Next, we opted to do antibiotic pills and a steroid capsule instead of the shot. It seemed to clear up most of the itching, but we still had to prevent the fleas from biting him.

I tried Bravecto, a three-in-one pill for fleas, ticks and heartworm control. Unfortunately, he was allergic to the medication and had a reaction to the pill. We did Trifexis, another three-way pill, and he vomited and stared at the ceiling while shaking. His vet later told me it was a seizure caused by yet another allergic reaction.

The topicals like Revolution do not work in our area anymore as the fleas have evolved to be unaffected, so those were out of the question. He couldn't have any more pills or internal medicines because he may be allergic, and I couldn't risk giving him another thing that may hurt him. I was out of options and desperate to help him feel better.

We eventually tried a fancy flea collar, one that lasts for eight months. It's called Seresto and it helped him tremendously.

Once we got him on Seresto, we steam cleaned everything in the house. Washed all the clothes, towels and bedding we owned, vacuumed and shampooed the carpets and furniture. We took away every opportunity for a flea or its larvae to have been inadvertently left behind and start the problem all over again.

Eventually, he healed. His hair began to regrow, his skin healed and went from raw and bleeding to smooth and new, almost like an infant. He got frequent baths, much to his dismay.

As I write this now, I can tell the warmer weather is on its way soon; Milo is beginning to flake. He gets dandruff from dry skin in the warmer months, leading him to itch himself silly until we end up right back where we were.

Thankfully through trial and error, I know how to care for his skin and keep it healthy. I know how to combat his allergies before they get out of control and leave him bald and in pain, and I know how to moisturize his skin properly to ensure less flaking and itching.

Having a dog with many allergies is not ideal, and it sure isn't easy. But Milo has always been worth it, even when it got expensive and heartbreaking to treat. We were at the vet six times in as many weeks, I cried constantly because all I wanted to do was make him better and I just couldn't.

Every time he scratches an itch, I flinch a little. Maybe it's some mild form of PTSD or something, but the simplest of itches has me on guard and worried for the next meltdown.

I'm hopeful that this year won't be nearly as rough on us because we did all the hard stuff last summer. We know what he's allergic to, and we know what just doesn't work, so I'm hoping those skills keep us from the disaster we faced last year.

OTIS RUNS AWAY

Otis runs, that's what he does. His Beagle nose gets a scent of something and he's off like a rocket. He doesn't know where he's going, and he doesn't know why he needs to, but his nose pulls him across the street, through traffic, and four miles away before he looks up and realizes he's not at home anymore, and I'm not with him.

Like any good hunter, Otis sniffs out his prey. And by prey, I mean he sniffs out a barbecue grill from miles away. He can smell a rack of ribs, a steak, and BBQ chicken three blocks down the road, and before you know it, his little legs have carried him in search of dinner.

One day, it was late February or early March, I can't remember for certain, he had the itch to run. The maintenance men let him out of the door when they came in to adjust the furnace, and off he went.

I followed closely behind wearing pajama pants, a hoodie, no bra and no shoes or socks. I followed him to the cemetery across the street and chased him barefoot through the gravestones. I called his name and yelled vague threats riddled with obscenities as he darted in front of cars and bikes. And after about a half an hour, I stopped and cried at the realization that he had never been gone this long, I couldn't find him, and he may never be coming back.

I had an aunt, a brother, and multiple friends out looking. I called the animal control office and the police station and gave his description and told them to call me if he was spotted or called about. Then, I headed home to put shoes on to protect my feet from the still frozen Michigan ground.

When I came home, my neighbor was sitting outside with a very happy Otis. Imagine my shock considering this was a dog who didn't like humans or being touched, and here he was, sitting tucked under the arm of a stranger.

I told her I'd been running all over and trying to find him. I detailed my journey to her and ended by asking where it was that she found him.

Turns out, Otis went on a run all right. Right to the neighbor downstairs, through her front door, and straight to the dish of cat food where he ate like I'd been starving him for months. This is where I roll my eyes, if you hadn't noticed.

I carried my fugitive home and he spent the next four hours hiding his head underneath the pillows and refusing to acknowledge me or my existence. He decidedly could not see me, could not hear me, and did not want anything to do with me. I won't lie; I didn't mind the little peace and quiet that his silent treatment allotted me.

Eventually he came around and stopped punishing me for him running off, and I wish I could say he never ran off again. But we all know Otis and we all know better. He did run, he ran far. I chased him, yelled and cursed at him, and every single time, I brought him home with me.

No matter how many times he runs, I swear to chase him. I promised him a good life, and I'm determined

Jeccika Shepherd

to give that to him, regardless of how
he feels about the situation.

THANK YOU

(Epilogue)

I don't know how to convey the surreal feeling that comes from writing this book. I grew up in a town with a couple thousand people, and now I write to more than that.

People from all over the world have followed our story and taken time from their lives to read what I have to say. People have told me they make a point to check the blog daily just to see what the boys are up to.

I've met some of the best people in the world by doing this, and I hope you get as much out of this as I do. Your support and love and unending kindness never goes unnoticed, and even a writer such as myself has trouble conveying the overwhelming feeling I get from doing what I do.

To open myself and my life up to strangers on the internet, to share my dogs and all their problems, to openly admit that while I always love them, I often don't like them, and for all of that to be met with positivity and support, it honestly leaves me speechless.

I don't know if you guys realize how rare and amazing the community we've built together is. We don't argue or call names. We don't debate and cut each other down. It's all so supportive and loving and so special. It's unlike anything I've ever seen before, and I'm so honored to have been a part of it.

It's hard to believe we've been doing this for almost three years, and it all started with a baked potato. I started talking to a handful of people, and my words weren't seen by thousands. I made my first post the day before I turned twenty-five, and in about a month, I'll be twenty-eight, and here I am, writing a book.

There's a breathtaking moment that comes when you realize how far your reach has gone. It never gets old seeing the comments, and still to this day, I read every single one. I know your dogs' names and your children as well. I know where you're from, who's a foster fail, who has naughty dogs like mine, and who's watch as you clean up their vomit.

It may sound weird or a little as-suming, but I think of all of you as friends and family to me, Joe and the boys. We know your names, your pic-tures, and your stories, and sometimes it's like talking to old friends.

I know it's pretty surreal for ya'll, too. You found a cute picture of a dog, it lured you in, and suddenly you're invested in a girl and her dogs in Michigan. I'm sure you never imagined you'd be wondering, "I wonder how Otis is doing since eating that sock," and I'm sure you didn't plan on celebrating with arms raised high when Milo lost his first thirteen pounds on thyroid medication.

But you did. And for that, I am so thankful. You've cried with us, celebrated with us, laughed and rolled your eyes with us. You've shared with us, talked to us, confided in us, and kept us updated as you grew through what you went through.

From a girl who had virtually no friends growing up to a woman who has made thousands of friends worldwide, I thank you.

I've never known such a feeling of comradery and acceptance. I've never felt such support and undying love before. There's no way to properly thank you for all the times you've been a friend, a confidante, a sounding board, and a support system.

When me and Joe decided to get married, the friends I have made on Michigan Juju were the first to send cards, the first to congratulate, and I think more excited than I was. In investing in the story of Milo and Otis, you've inadvertently invested in me, too, and I'm so humbled and grateful for you.

For all the times I've made you laugh, made you cry, or made you think, you've stuck it out with me, and

I never imagined being here, writing the ending to our first book.

I always pictured the first book I wrote to be lengthy and nearly a novel. However, as I wrote this, I found myself keeping it short and simple, the same way I do with the blog daily. I didn't want our style and our message to get lost just for the sake of making the book longer. As I wrote, the emotion was receding, and the writing felt stiff and unnatural.

So here it is, in all it's glory. Shorter than we planned, but full of love and some of the best stories of the boys and their antics. I saved some for book two, but with their naughty selves, I'm sure I can fill a whole series.

From the bottom of my heart, I want to thank you all for buying this book. For reading what I have to say, and for caring about a girl and her dogs. For those who encouraged me to write this, I thank you. For those who believed in me before I could believe in myself, I thank you. And for being the good in the world, I thank you.

Now, for the first time in print, I have one last thing to say to you:

Love and good juju from Michigan.

32450757R00068

Made in the USA
Lexington, KY
02 March 2019